LIFE CYCLES

# The Life Cycle of Reptiles

Darlene R. Stille

Heinemann
LIBRARY

Chicago, Illinois

## www.heinemannraintree.com

Visit our website to find out more information about Heinemann-Raintree books.

## To order:

☎ Phone 888-454-2279

▣ Visit www.heinemannraintree.com to browse our catalog and order online.

© 2012 Heinemann Library
an imprint of Capstone Global Library, LLC
Chicago, Illinois

Edited by Abby Colich, Megan Cotugno, and Kate de Villiers
Designed by Victoria Allen
Illustrated by Darren Lingard
Picture research by Hannah Taylor
Originated by Capstone Global Library, Ltd.
Printed and bound in China by CTPS

14 13 12 11
10 9 8 7 6 5 4 3 2 1

**Library of Congress Cataloging-in-Publication Data**
Stille, Darlene R.
  The life cycle of reptiles / Darlene Stille.
    p. cm.—(Life cycles)
  Includes bibliographical references and index.
  ISBN 978-1-4329-4982-2 (hc)—ISBN 978-1-4329-4989-1
(pb)  1. Reptiles—Life cycles—Juvenile literature.  I. Title.
  QL644.2.S754 2012
  597.9'156—dc22                    2010038507

**Acknowledgments**
The author and publisher are grateful to the following for permission to reproduce copyright material: © Corbis: pp. 15 (© Brian J. Skerry/National Geographic Society), 28 (© DLILLC); © Photolibrary: pp. 13 (Animals Animals/Jim Tuten), 14 (Animals Animals/Joe McDonald), 17 (Animals Animals/John Cancalosi), 26 (Imagebroker.net/JW.Alker), 29 (Age Fotostock/John Cancalosi), 31 (OSF/Werner Bollmann), 33 top (Animals Animals/David M Dennis), 34 (Imagebroker. net/jspix ), 39 (Peter Arnold Images/Jeffrey L. Rotman); © Photoshot: pp. 35 (© NHPA), 38 (© NHPA); © Shutterstock: pp. 4 (© Uryadnikov Sergey), 5 (© Rich Carey), 6 (© Scott Payne), 8 (© Elizabeth Spencer), 9 (© Uryadnikov Sergey), 10 (© Eduardo Rivero), 11 (© Julian W), 16 (© Heiko Kiera), 21 (© FikMik), 23 (© Kjersti Joergensen), 24 (© Eugene Buchko), 25 (© Dirk Ercken), 27 (© Jungleboy), 33 bottom (© Jason Mintzer), 37 (© Ryan M. Bolton).

Cover photograph of a Komodo Dragon on a beach in Komodo National Park reproduced with permission of © Corbis (© Visuals Unlimited).

We would like to thank Dr. Michael Bright for his invaluable help in the preparation of this book.

Every effort has been made to contact copyright holders of any material reproduced in this book. Any omissions will be rectified in subsequent printings if notice is given to the publisher.

# Contents

Some words are shown in bold, **like this**. You can find out what they mean by looking in the glossary.

**Look but don't touch:** Many reptiles are easily hurt. If you see one in the wild, do not get too close to it. Look at it, but do not try to touch it!

# What Is a Reptile?

Reptiles make up a huge group of animals. There are more than 8,700 **species,** or kinds, of reptiles. Reptiles live everywhere except the coldest places on Earth, near the north and south poles. There is no way to count all the reptiles living on the planet.

## Groups of reptiles

Alligators, crocodiles, snakes, lizards, and turtles are all reptiles. Wormlike **amphisbaenians** and lizard-like **tuataras** are also reptiles. These types of animals are reptiles because they all have certain traits, or characteristics.

**Biologists** group, or classify, animals by the traits that they share. All reptiles are **vertebrates**. Vertebrates are animals with backbones. All reptiles have lungs to get oxygen from the air. All reptiles have dry, scaly skin. All reptiles, except the leatherback turtle, are cold-blooded. They cannot warm or cool their bodies. They must depend on the temperatures outside. Leatherbacks are **gigantotherms**. They use the large size of their bodies to warm up or cool down in warm or cool seas.

A snake has a long, dry, scaly body. It does not have legs.

## Were Dinosaurs Reptiles?

Scientists classify **extinct** dinosaurs as reptiles. Dinosaurs shared many traits with reptiles of today. Some prehistoric reptiles, however, may have been warm-blooded instead of cold-blooded. They may have been able to control their body temperature. Dinosaurs roamed Earth during the Mesozoic era (also called "the age of reptiles") from about 250 million to 65 million years ago.

The green sea turtle spends almost its entire life underwater.

# What Kinds of Reptiles Are There?

There are reptiles that walk and reptiles that swim. There are reptiles that slither on their bellies. **Biologists** sort reptiles into four main groups:

- lizards, **amphisbaenians**, and snakes
- turtles and tortoises
- crocodilians
- tuataras.

## Lizards, amphisbaenians, and snakes

The largest reptile group is made up of lizards, **amphisbaenians**, and snakes. Lizards come in many colors, shapes, and sizes. Some small lizards look like snakes because they do not have legs. Some big lizards look like crocodiles.

The collared lizard has two black bands that look like collars around its neck.

Amphisbaenians, or worm lizards, look like earthworms. They burrow in the ground. Unlike worms, amphisbaenians have bony skulls and powerful jaws.

Snakes have long bodies without legs. Their scales can have many colors. Snakes have a keen (sharp) sense of smell. They flick out their long, forked tongues to smell odors. They do not see or hear very well.

## Where Do Reptiles "Belong"?

Scientists group living things by how they are alike or different. All animals go into one big group called the animal kingdom. The next group is called the phylum. Reptiles fit into the phylum Chordata. All animals with backbones belong to Chordata. Next come a smaller group called the class. All reptiles belong to the class Reptilia. Biologists keep sorting reptiles into smaller and smaller groups, including order, family, genus, and **species**.

There are four main groups of reptiles. The chart shows some of the kinds of reptiles that fit into each group.

| lizards, amphisbaenians, and snakes | turtles | crocodilians | tuataras |
|---|---|---|---|
| Gila monsters | tortoises | alligators | tuataras |
| rattlesnakes | box turtles | American crocodiles | |
| cobras | terrapins | Nile crocodiles | |
| amphisbaenians | leatherback sea turtles | saltwater crocodiles | |
| geckos | snapping turtles | caimans | |
| skinks | soft-shelled turtles | gavials | |
| iguanas | | | |

# Turtles and tortoises

Most turtles have a hard shell that acts like armor. The shell is made of two layers. The layer next to the turtle is part of its **skeleton**. The outer layer of hard-shelled turtles is made of **scutes**. Scutes are a hard material like that of horns. The outer shell layer of soft-shelled turtles is made of very tough skin.

Turtle shells have a top and a bottom. The top, or **carapace**, covers the turtle's back. The bottom, or **plastron**, covers the turtle's underside. A bony bridge joins the two parts.

A box turtle can completely close its hinged shell.

The powerful Komodo dragon is the largest lizard.

Some turtles live in freshwater and others live in salt water. Freshwater turtles in the British Isles are called **terrapins**. Tortoises live on land. Small mud turtles and musk turtles live in shallow, muddy water. Box turtles live mainly on land. They have a dome-shaped carapace. Their plastron has a hinge. A box turtle can close up its shell like a box.

### The Biggest Lizard

Komodo dragons may look scary to some people. They can weigh up to 165 kilograms (365 pounds). They can kill deer, pigs, and water buffalo with their sharp claws and teeth. These lizards live in Indonesia.

Snapping turtles have powerful beaks. Like all turtles, they lack teeth. They use their sharp beaks to catch food and defend themselves. Sea turtles live in the ocean. They are the biggest turtles. A leatherback turtle can weigh 900 kilograms (2,000 pounds)!

# Crocodilians

The third main group of reptiles is called crocodilians. This group includes alligators, crocodiles, caimans, and gavials.

Alligators have big, long bodies with short legs and powerful tails. They use their legs for walking. They use their tails and webbed feet for swimming. Alligators have big jaws with many sharp teeth. Their eyes are on top of their heads so they can see above water when swimming. Males are bigger than females. Male alligators can be 3.7 meters (12 feet) long and weigh up to 249 kilograms (550 pounds).

Crocodiles look a lot like alligators, but they have differently shaped noses. Crocodiles have longer, pointy noses than the rounded noses of alligators. The jaws and teeth of alligators and crocodiles also look different. Crocodiles have a bottom tooth that sticks up over their upper lips. A male crocodile can grow up to 5.5 meters (18 feet) long.

This is an American crocodile in Costa Rica.

The lizard-like tuatara sits on a forest floor in New Zealand.

There are more crocodiles than caimans. Some caimans are smaller than alligators and crocodiles. Males grow to 2.4 meters (8 feet). The spectacled caiman has bony ridges around its eyes. They look like glasses, or spectacles.

Gavials look like crocodiles with long, narrow snouts. They are about 5.5 meters (18 feet) long. These endangered animals live in only a few areas, such as Bangladesh and India.

## Tuataras

There are only two species of **tuataras**. These lizard-like reptiles live on islands off New Zealand.

# How Is a Reptile Born?

## Born from eggs

Most baby reptiles hatch from eggs. Crocodilian babies hatch from eggs with hard shells. Animals that hatch from eggs outside the mother's body are called **oviparous**.

## Snake and croc eggs

Most reptiles that lay eggs just leave them. Pythons are one of the few reptiles that protect their eggs. Female pythons coil their bodies around the eggs until they hatch.

Alligators and crocodiles stay near the nest to guard their eggs. They also provide some care for the babies after they hatch. Mother alligators help the babies climb out of the nest. They watch over their young for about a year. Mother crocodiles pick up the babies with their mouths and carry them to the nearest water.

### The Egg Tooth

Baby reptiles that hatch from a hard shell must break out on their own. To help crack the shell, they grow a special "tooth" called an egg tooth. This tooth is tough enough to crack the shell from the inside. The egg tooth grows on the snouts of baby alligators and crocodiles.

# Born live

Some snakes and lizards are born live. The eggs hatch inside the mother's body. The babies do not get food from the mother's body. Animals born this way are called **ovoviviparous**. Some snakes and lizards get food from the mother while they grow inside her body. Animals that nourish and give birth to live babies are called **viviparous**.

A hatching alligator uses its egg tooth to help break out of its shell.

## Turtle eggs

Baby turtles grow inside eggs that are buried in the ground. Adult turtles do not guard the nests. Often, skunks, raccoons, and snakes dig up and eat the eggs.

Like other reptile eggs, turtle eggs must be heated from outside. The heat usually comes from the Sun. Whether the baby turtle is male or female depends on how warm the nest gets. In some turtle **species**, warmer temperatures create more female babies.

Baby turtles use an egg tooth to break out of their shells. Newly hatched turtles are called **hatchlings**. The hatchlings must dig their way out of the ground.

A female garter snake gives birth to live young.

Turtle hatchlings claw their way out of an underground nest.

The hatchlings then must find their own food and protect themselves. They face many dangers. Tortoise and freshwater turtle hatchlings become dinner for birds, bullfrogs, snakes, and even other turtles. Sea turtle hatchlings must run across beaches from their nests to the sea. On the way, birds and all kinds of land animals often eat them. Once the baby sea turtles reach the water, fish eat even more of them.

Snake eggs have leathery shells. As the baby snakes grow bigger, the egg shells expand. The baby snakes use a kind of egg tooth to slit open the shells. Some female sea snakes give birth to live young. The young are born underwater. Like other reptiles, most lizards hatch from eggs laid in nests. But some species give birth to live young.

# How Do Reptiles Grow?

Reptiles grow in different ways. Some growing reptiles get rid of their old skin and get new skin!

## Young snakes

A snake has two layers of scaly skin. As the first layer dies, it pushes up to form an outer layer. The growing snake sheds its outer layer. Shedding skin is called **molting**. Snakes grow fastest when they are young and molt more often. But they grow and molt all of their lives. Sometimes older snakes molt because their skin is just worn out and they need a new one.

Until age three or four, American alligators have yellow bands around their dark bodies.

## Young crocs and alligators

Young crocodiles sometimes get help from their mothers. Some female crocodiles help the little crocodiles hatch. The mother then carries the babies in her mouth. She places them in a river or other body of water. She watches over the growing crocodiles for about one year.

Newborn alligators are about 23 centimeters (9 inches) long. For six or seven years, they grow about 30 centimeters (12 inches) a year. Both males and females reach adulthood between 10 and 12 years of age.

**How Snakes Molt**

A snake begins to molt, or **slough** its skin, by rubbing its nose on a rock or other rough surface. The rubbing loosens the skin around its head and mouth. The snake then starts to crawl out of its skin, turning the skin inside out.

A snake starts to molt by loosening the skin around its head.

# Young lizards and turtles

Most young lizards are ready to find food and shelter as soon as they are born. They get no help from adult lizards.

A few mother lizards do care for their eggs. Some kinds of **skinks** keep their eggs warm with their bodies. Some skinks are born live, but the babies are ready to be on their own right away.

As lizards grow, they grow out of their skin. Almost all lizards cast off their old skins in pieces. But the glass snake, a kind of lizard, sheds its skin in once piece as snakes do. Lizards grow up faster than crocodilians. Geckos become adults in about a year. It takes an iguana two years to be a fully grown adult. **Prairie** skinks become adults when they are about three years old.

Turtles grow with their shells. All turtles, young and old, have shells attached to their backs. Unlike a snake, a turtle cannot shed its shell. When a hard-shelled turtle grows, its shell must grow with it. As the shell grows, it sheds **scutes**. Smaller, older scutes fall off. The shell grows new, bigger scutes.

### A Baby Sea Turtle Grows Up

As soon as it hatches, a baby sea turtle heads for the water. To escape hungry fish and other sea animals, the turtle starts to swim as fast as it can. It swims for up to two days to reach deep water. There are fewer **predators** there. The young turtle stays in deep water and grows for 5 to 10 years.

Old scutes that make up the outer layer of a hard turtle shell fall off and are replaced by bigger scutes.

new scute

old scute

# How Do Reptiles Move Around?

Some reptiles swim, some crawl, some walk, some glide, and some run fast. In the prehistoric age, there were even flying reptiles called pterosaurs.

## Crocodilians can move fast

Alligators, crocodiles, caimans, and gavials are better swimmers than runners. They float with only their eyes above the surface. They wait for **prey** and then suddenly attack. An alligator or crocodile can swim up to 32 kilometers per hour (20 miles per hour). They can run short distances at speeds of about 18 kilometers per hour (11 miles per hour).

## Lizard movement methods

Different kinds of lizards move in a variety of ways. Lizards that lack legs wiggle over the ground like snakes. **Tuataras** and lizards with legs run. Some lizards, such as the Australian frilled lizard, can run on their back legs.

Geckos live mainly in trees. They have claws and sticky pads on their feet. The pads let geckos cling to smooth surfaces. A gecko can walk up a glass window!

Flying dragons that live in Asia have flaps of skin on their sides that they can spread. They use the flaps as wings to glide from tree to tree.

## Staying Still

During cold winters, reptiles **hibernate**. The reptile's body grows cold. It does not need food because it uses little energy. It looks like it is asleep. The tuatara can stand cold weather. Desert reptiles **estivate** during hot, dry summers. Estivation protects against dry weather the way hibernation protects against cold.

Sticky foot pads let a gecko walk up smooth surfaces.

# Slither and wriggle

Sea snakes swim by moving their tails. Snakes that live on land have four main ways of moving.

In one way of moving, a snake's body forms "S" curves as it goes forward. The snake curves its body from side to side. **Biologists** call this slithering motion "lateral undulation."

A snake can also creep along the ground. First the scales on its belly move forward and catch on rough surfaces. The snake then pushes against the scales to move its whole body forward. Biologists call this motion "rectilinear movement."

**Concertina** movement looks like an accordion or concertina being pulled open and squeezed shut. The snake bends its body, pulls the front part forward, then pushes the back part toward the front.

Some desert snakes use a **sidewinder** movement to go through loose, dry soil. The snake throws the middle part of its body sideways. It then brings its head and tail to where its body is.

# Moving skin

Loose skin surrounds the wormlike bodies of **amphisbaenians**. An amphisbaenian can move through a dirt burrow by keeping its body straight and making its skin ripple. It can also use a concertina movement.

### Snakes and Water

Some snakes live on land and some snakes live in water. But all snakes can swim—even rattlesnakes that live in desert areas.

Sea turtles paddle with front flippers.

## Feet and paddles

Turtles that live on land walk on short, stubby legs and feet. Freshwater turtles use webbed feet for swimming. Sea turtles paddle through the ocean with flippers, instead of feet, on their front legs.

# Where Do Reptiles Live?

Reptiles live everywhere except the coldest places on Earth. There are no reptiles in Antarctica or in the Arctic Ocean. Some reptiles only live on land, and others live in water.

## Desert reptiles

More lizards and snakes live in the deserts of the southwestern United States than any other large animal. Hikers in the Mojave, Sonoran, and Colorado deserts might see a desert iguana or a desert spiny lizard. Desert iguanas escape the heat by hiding in burrows. The desert spiny lizard takes cover in rocks.

The horned lizard lives in deserts.

The western diamondback rattlesnake makes its home in the Colorado Desert. **Sidewinders**, king snakes, and red racers also live in this dry land.

Desert reptiles have **adaptations** that help them survive. Some get water without drinking from ponds or streams. The thorny devil lizard of Australia has pointy scales. Tiny grooves in the scales collect dew and send it to the lizard's mouth. The desert tortoise spends most of its life underground to keep cool.

## Forest reptiles

Many snakes live in tropical rain forests. Australia's brown and green tree snakes glide along trunks and branches. Some rain forest snakes, such as the boa constrictors of South America and pythons of Southeast Asia, are huge. Geckos and chameleons are among the rain forest lizards.

Timber rattlesnakes live in dense forests in the eastern United States. The rattles on their tails give off a warning buzz to anyone who comes too close.

Asian and South American rain forests are home to huge snakes.

## Pasture and prairie

Reptiles live on open lands. In the British Isles, the grass snake, European adder, and common lizard live in **prairie**-like areas called **heathland**. The Great Plains **skink** and other lizards live on the prairies of the midwestern United States. Two kinds of box turtles and the harmless rat snake also live on the Great Plains.

## Water-dwelling reptiles

Sea snakes and sea turtles live in the ocean. Most sea snakes have nostrils on top of their heads so they can float and breathe air. Sea snakes can close their nostrils to keep out salt water when they dive deep. Sea turtles live mainly in warm oceans around the equator. Leatherback turtles **migrate** to warmer waters for **breeding**.

Banded sea kraits deliver a deadly bite.

Crocodilians lurk in muddy water.

**Gator Holes**

Winter is the dry season in Florida's Everglades, a swampy grassland area. Many birds, fish, mammals, and even plants find water in gator holes. Alligators dig these holes in soft rock under the soil. The holes fill with water and make a place for many creatures to spend the winter.

Most freshwater snakes live in warm places. Anacondas live in rivers of South America. Black **swamp** snakes and water moccasins, or cottonmouths, live in swamps in the southeastern United States.

Crocodiles lurk in swamps and muddy rivers in Australia, southern Florida, Central America, Africa, India, South America, and Southeast Asia. Alligators live in the United States and China. Caimans are found in Central and South America. Gavials live in and around India.

# What Do Reptiles Eat?

The reptile menu lists many foods. Some reptiles just eat animals. Others only eat plants. Still others eat pretty much whatever they find.

## Animal eaters

All snakes and most other reptiles are **carnivores**. They only eat other animals.

Some lizards, snakes, and turtles eat insects. Chameleons, lizards that live in Africa, catch insects with their long, sticky tongues. The Texas blind snake eats ants and termites. Some baby turtles mainly eat insects. **Amphisbaenians** capture insects and worms in their powerful jaws.

Some turtles only eat plants.

**Tuataras** of New Zealand are night hunters. They use their sharp teeth to tear apart birds, **amphibians**, snails, and smaller lizards.

**Gila monsters** of the Sonoran Desert gobble birds, eggs, frogs, small mammals, and other lizards. They eat three or four huge meals a year and store the extra calories as fat. Big Komodo dragons are powerful enough to capture and eat deer, pigs, and even water buffalo.

Alligators and crocodiles sneak up on **prey** and grab the animal in their powerful jaws. They swallow birds, fish, frogs, and turtles whole. Alligators drown large animals. The crocodile spins to rip chunks of meat off the animal.

## Plant eaters

A few reptiles are **herbivores**, or plant eaters. One of the biggest sea turtles is a plant eater. Weighing up to 318 kilograms (700 pounds), the green sea turtle grazes on sea grasses and algae. Freshwater turtles, such as peninsula cooters, also eat plants. The green iguana and the chuckwalla are among the few plant-eating lizards.

A lizard grabs a small animal in its mouth.

# Reptile omnivores

A reptile that eats plants or animals is called an **omnivore**. Many turtles are omnivores. Olive ridley sea turtles will eat seaweed if the sea creatures it usually eats are scarce. They use their powerful jaws to crack and grind up the shells of crabs, mollusks, and shrimp.

The snapping turtle is a freshwater turtle that eats whatever comes along. It snaps its jaws shut on frogs, birds, small mammals, and smaller turtles. It grabs insects, worms, and snails. It eats all kinds of water plants. The red-eared **terrapin**, which was brought to the British Isles from the United States, is also an omnivore.

The bearded dragon is an omnivorous lizard. It lives on dry lands in Australia, where food may be difficult to find. Bearded dragons have big stomachs, which they fill with plants, insects, spiders, rodents, and other lizards.

# Changing habits

The foods that some reptiles eat change as the reptiles grow older. Slider turtles like to eat more animals than plants when they are young. As the sliders get older, they eat more plants than animals.

### Picky Eaters

Some reptiles will eat only one kind of food. Common egg-eating snakes of southern Africa only eat birds' eggs. The leatherback sea turtle only eats squid and jellyfish. The Hawksbill turtle has a long, thin, birdlike beak that lets it pull its favorite food, **sponges**, from cracks in coral reefs.

The body of a python bulges after the snake swallows a large animal.

# How Do Reptiles Protect Themselves?

Snakes, lizards, and turtles need to watch out for birds, mammals, and other reptiles. Reptiles have many ways of protecting themselves against **predators**.

## Hiding out

Small reptiles have a better chance of not being eaten if they hide rather than fight. Many lizards have colors that help them fade into the background. Spiny lizards of the western United States are gray or brown with dark patterns to help them blend in with the desert rocks and soil. Grass snakes of the British Isles are green to blend in with the green, wooded area they slither through.

Turtles and other reptiles that live in water have dark backs and light bellies. A dark back makes them harder to spot from above. The light belly blends in with the bright sky, which makes them harder to spot from below.

Other reptiles stay in burrows during the day. They come out to eat at night when they are harder to see.

## Wearing a disguise

Some harmless reptiles disguise themselves as dangerous ones. Wearing this kind of disguise is called **mimicry**. The harmless king snake has color patterns that look like those of the deadly coral snake.

Some harmless reptiles behave like dangerous ones. The harmless bull snake, or gopher snake, acts like a rattlesnake when threatened. It lifts its head and hisses. It shakes its tail in dried leaves or grass to make a rattling sound.

The red, black, and yellow or white bands of the harmless king snake (below) might scare off enemies, because they look a lot like those of the dangerous coral snake (top).

## Changing colors

The chameleon is a lizard that can change colors to communicate and control its body temperature.

Anoles are another kind of lizard that can change colors. One kind of anole lives in the southern United States. The others live in Central and South America.

## Wearing armor

Turtles use their shells for protection. Many turtles can pull their heads and legs inside the shell. They wait for the danger to pass.

Crocs and some lizards have armor-like scales. The tough scales of horned lizards and the pointed scales of the thorny devil lizard are difficult for predators to bite through.

The scary-looking Australian frilled lizard unfurls loose skin around its neck.

A male saltwater crocodile defends its territory by fighting off an invading male.

## Strange defenses

Some snakes and lizards try to look scary. The Australian frilled lizard has a flap of loose skin around its head. When it feels threatened, this lizard stands on its hind legs, opens its mouth wide, spreads out the skin flap, and hisses.

The Texas horned lizard can squirt blood from its eyes! It seems animals that **prey** on it do not like the taste of its blood.

Many lizards can break off their tails if an enemy grabs the tail. The lizards then grow new tails.

# Are Reptiles Dangerous to People?

Reptiles attack only if they feel threatened. A few reptiles can harm people. Some lizards and some snakes can even kill people. The big teeth and jaws of alligators and other crocodilians can cause serious injuries.

## Snake dangers

The bite of snakes that have teeth can hurt. Snakes that carry poison called **venom** can cause great harm. All rattlesnakes inject venom through their fangs when they bite. Anyone bitten by a rattlesnake must go to a hospital emergency room.

The most deadly snakes are coral snakes, mambas, tiger snakes, taipans, and brown snakes. Cobras can bite or spit venom accurately enough to blind a person.

Constrictors kill by wrapping themselves around an animal and squeezing it so it cannot breathe. Constrictors include anacondas, boas, and pythons. A big constrictor could **suffocate** a person.

## Dangerous lizards

Until recently, **biologists** knew of just two venomous lizards—the **Gila monster** of the Southwest and the Mexican beaded lizard. New studies show that the Komodo dragon also injects poison into its victims. Komodo dragons are big and powerful enough to injure or kill people.

## Drugs from Venom

Researchers study reptile venom and look for ways to make drugs. They have made a drug from the Brazilian arrowhead viper to lower blood pressure. Venom of the southeastern pygmy rattlesnake led to a new heart disease treatment. The venom of the Gila monster could lead to a new diabetes drug.

A coiled rattlesnake hisses and the rattles on its tail make a buzzing sound to warn off enemies.

# How Do Reptiles Reproduce?

Most reptiles **reproduce** sexually. Male sperm, or sex cells, unite with female eggs. The uniting of sperm and egg is called **fertilization**. Most reptiles are **oviparous**, which means they lay eggs in nests. Some are **viviparous**. They feed the unborn babies inside their bodies, similar to the way mammals do. Others are **ovoviviparous**, so the eggs hatch inside the mother.

## Croc mating

**Breeding** is a noisy business for alligators and crocodiles. Males stake out a territory in shallow water. They call to females by roaring. April and May is the mating season for American alligators and crocodiles. Males deposit sperm inside females. Females then lay the fertilized eggs in nests built above the water.

Crocodilians in other parts of the world breed at different times of the year. Mating among caimans and gavials is much like that of alligators and crocodiles. All crocodilians are oviparous.

A crocodilian female lays fertilized eggs in a nest.

# Lizard reproduction

**Monitors**, horned lizards, some **skinks**, and most other kinds of lizards lay eggs. A few lizard **species** are viviparous and some are ovoviviparous. The common lizard in the British Isles and other European countries is viviparous. The northern alligator lizard is one of the few ovoviviparous lizards.

Some kinds of lizards do not reproduce sexually. New Mexico whiptail lizards are all female. Several species of whiptails have no males. The females lay eggs. Only female whiptails hatch from the eggs. All the **hatchlings** are identical to their mother.

Olive Ridley sea turtles return to land to lay their eggs.

## Turtles bury eggs

All turtles reproduce sexually and are oviparous. Males fertilize eggs inside the females. All turtles lay their eggs on land.

Females of most turtle species dig a hole. After laying the eggs, the turtle covers them with dirt, sand, or rotting plant parts. One kind of tortoise lays only one egg. Some sea turtles lay up to 200 eggs.

## Snake eggs

All snakes reproduce sexually, and most snakes lay eggs. Many females might lay eggs in the same place. They lay them in holes in the ground or holes in logs or tree stumps. Females of only a few species, such as some pythons and cobras, stay to guard the eggs.

Some snakes give birth to live babies. Some of these snakes, such as garter snakes, brown snakes, copperheads, cottonmouths, and rattlesnakes, are ovoviviparous. A few snake species, such as Australia's northern death adder, are viviparous.

### Long Journeys Home

Even though they live in the ocean, sea turtles lay their eggs on land. The females of all seven kinds of sea turtles return to the beach where they were born. Some turtles travel hundreds or thousands of miles. Males go with them. They mate just off the beaches. Only the females go up on the beach. They dig holes, lay their eggs, and then return to the ocean again.

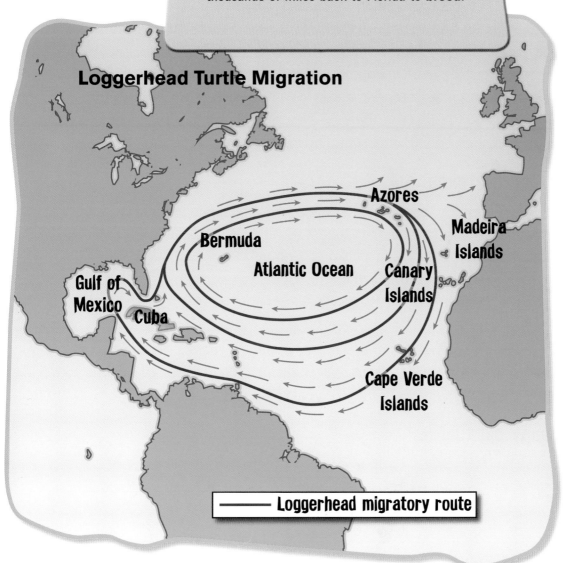

Some loggerhead turtles leave Florida beaches to spend their lives riding **currents** around the Atlantic Ocean. They travel thousands of miles back to Florida to **breed**.

## Loggerhead Turtle Migration

Azores

Madeira Islands

Bermuda

Atlantic Ocean

Canary Islands

Gulf of Mexico

Cuba

Cape Verde Islands

—— Loggerhead migratory route

# How Long Do Reptiles Live?

How long a reptile lives depends on what kind it is. Some snakes and lizards live just a few years. Crocodilians can live for decades, and turtles can live 100 years.

## Snake lifetimes

It is difficult for **biologists** to tell exactly how old snakes will live in the wild. However, they can track ages of snakes in captivity. Many snakes can live about 20 years in captivity. Bigger snakes may live longer than smaller snakes. The European adder lives about 15 years. The grass snake lives up to 25 years. Pythons live up to 35 years. The oldest known snake was a boa constrictor that died at age 40 in 1977.

## Lizard lifetimes

The lizard with the shortest **life span** is a rare chameleon that lives on Madagascar (a large island southeast of Africa). It lives only one year. Most chameleons live up to 10 years in zoos. The common lizard lives up to six years. **Gila monsters** live about 30 years in zoos.

## Old crocs

The Australian saltwater crocodile lives about 70 years. Nile crocodiles may live from 45 years to more than 80 years. The life span of alligators in the Everglades may be 50 to 60 years.

## Really old turtles

Turtles hold the record for the longest-lived reptiles. Some kinds of box turtles can live at least 100 years. Some tortoises have life spans of more than 150 years!

Life cycles of snakes, crocs, turtles, most lizards, and other reptiles begin with a **fertilized** egg that hatches into a baby. The young reptile looks like a small adult. When grown, males and females mate to produce fertilized eggs.

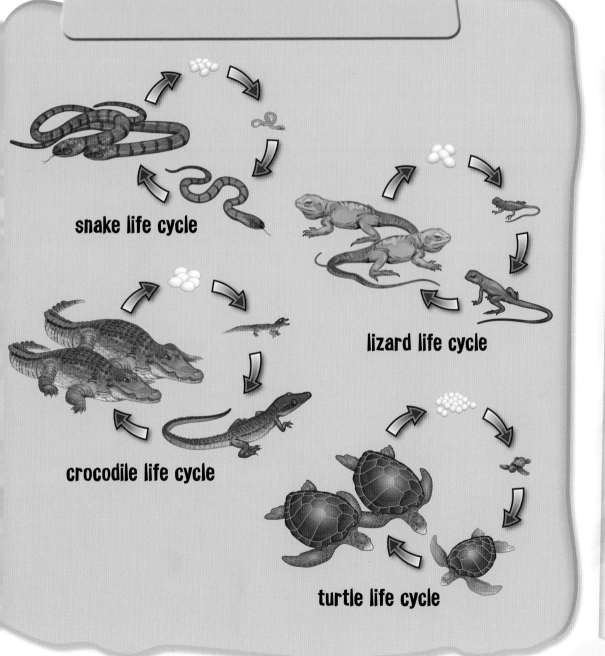

snake life cycle

lizard life cycle

crocodile life cycle

turtle life cycle

# Reptile Facts

The largest reptile in size and weight is the saltwater crocodile. These crocs can be about 6 meters (20 feet) long and weigh more than 544 kilograms (1,200 pounds).

Reptiles have day or night **pupils**. Reptiles that are active after dark have pupils that look like slits. Reptiles that are active during daylight have round pupils.

The Mesozoic era, about 250 million to 65 million years ago, was called "the age of reptiles." During this time, dinosaurs, which were huge reptiles, roamed Earth.

The largest Komodo dragon (a kind of large lizard called a **monitor**) ever measured was 3 meters (9.8 feet) long and weighed about 166 kilograms (365 pounds).

If an enemy breaks off the tail of a lizard, the tail will keep wiggling to confuse the enemy. This gives the lizard time to get away.

The blue-tongued lizard of Australia flashes a bright blue tongue when it feels threatened.

The biggest snake **species** is the green anaconda of South America. Anacondas can grow to more than 8 meters (26 feet) long and weigh more than 227 kilograms (500 pounds).

The black mamba that lives in Africa may be the fastest-moving snake. It can travel at speeds of about 20 kilometers per hour (12.4 miles per hour).

The largest kind of turtle is the leatherback sea turtle. It grows up to 2.4 meters (7.9 feet) long and weighs about 907 kilograms (2,000 pounds).

Turtles can carry a germ called *salmonella* that can cause illness in humans. For this reason, turtles do not make good pets for small children.

# Glossary

**adaptation** change in an organism to help it live in a certain environment

**amphibian** animal that spends part of its life in water and part on land

**amphisbaenian** wormlike reptile

**biologist** scientist who studies living things

**breed** to produce offspring

**carapace** top of a turtle's shell that covers its back

**carnivore** animal that only eats meat

**concertina** musical instrument played by stretching and squeezing it

**current** body of water that moves in another body of water

**estivate** spend hot, dry summers in a sleeplike state

**extinct** no longer living

**fertilization** joining sperm with an egg so it can develop into a new animal

**gigantotherm** animal that uses its large, bulky body to control its body temperature

**Gila monster** venomous desert lizard

**hatchling** young animal that just hatched from an egg

**heathland** area of open, unfarmed land

**herbivore** animal that only eats plants

**hibernate** spend cold winters in a sleeplike state

**life span** period of time an animal might live

**migrate** to move from one place to another

**mimicry** to look like another dangerous animal

**molt** shed old skin

**monitor** a kind of lizard

**omnivore** animal that eats plants and meat

**oviparous** giving birth to young by laying eggs

**ovoviviparous** giving birth to babies that hatch from eggs inside the mother's body

**plastron** bottom of a turtle's shell that covers its belly

**prairie** area of open grassland

**predator** animal that hunts and eats another animal

**prey** animal that is hunted by another and killed for food; to hunt another animal

**pupil** dark circle at the center of eyes

**reproduce** to produce offspring

**scute** horny or bony plate on the shell of a turtle or the back of another kind of reptile

**sidewinder** rattlesnake that throws itself sideways

**skeleton** bones or other material that supports an animal's body

**skink** type of lizard with short legs

**slough** shed old skin

**species** group of similar organisms

**sponge** soft marine animal filled with holes

**suffocate** kill by cutting off air to an animal or person

**swamp** area of low, wet land

**terrapin** freshwater turtle in the British Isles

**tuatara** type of reptile found in New Zealand

**venom** poison injected by a snake when biting

**vertebrate** animal with a backbone

**viviparous** giving birth to live babies that have developed inside a mother's body

# Find Out More

## Books

Bredeson, Carmen. *Fun Facts About Turtles!* Berkeley, N.J.: Enslow, 2009.

Ganeri, Anita. *Anaconda*. Chicago: Heinemann Library, 2010.

Gibbons, Gail. *Snakes*. New York: Holiday House, 2010.

Haywood, Karen. *Crocodiles and Alligators*. New York: Benchmark Books, 2010.

## Websites

National Geographic Kids: Creature Features
http://kids.nationalgeographic.com/kids/animals/creaturefeature

National Marine Fisheries Service: Sea Turtles
www.nmfs.noaa.gov/pr/education/turtles.htm

Smithsonian National Zoological Park: Reptiles & Amphibians
http://nationalzoo.si.edu/Animals/ReptilesAmphibians/ForKids/default.cfm

# Index